Klaus Paysan

BIRDS OF THE WORLD

in field and garden

Lerner Publications Company
Minneapolis, Minnesota

The Library of Congress cataloged the original printing of this title as follows:

Paysan, Klaus.
  Birds of the world in field and garden. [Photos and text by] Klaus Paysan.
[Sketches by Angela Paysan. English translation by Jane Owen] Minneapolis,
Lerner Publications Co. [1970, c1968]
  112 p. illus. (part col.) 22 x 25 cm.
  Brief text and color photographs describe the physical characteristics and
habits of forty-two birds from all parts of the world.
  Translation of Vögel in Feld und Garten.
  1. Birds—Juvenile literature. 2. Birds—Pictorial works. [1. Birds] I. Paysan,
Angela, illus. II. Title.

QL676.P3513 1970	598.2	70-102891
ISBN 0-8225-0560-6		MARC
		A C

A NATURE AND MAN BOOK

Second Printing 1974

First published in the United States 1970 by Lerner Publications Company,
Minneapolis, Minnesota. All English language rights reserved.
Published simultaneously in Canada by J. M. Dent & Sons Ltd., Don Mills, Ontario.
Copyright © MCMLXVIII by Deutsche Verlags-Anstalt, Stuttgart, Germany.

International Standard Book Number: 0-8225-0560-6
Library of Congress Catalog Card Number: 70-102891

Manufactured in the United States of America.

CONTENTS

INTRODUCTION

Throughout the world man has had more contact with the bird than with any other wild creature. He has made a careful study of birds and their habits, and has found that there are many different species of birds, as well as many varieties of the same species. A bird can be distinguished from others of the same species by paying careful attention to its special characteristics of song, coloring, living areas, and breeding habits.

Some varieties of birds live in areas throughout the world, while others live in only one or two countries. Some birds have the same name as a bird in another country, but are not even a member of the same species. For example, the European blackbird and the European robin are different birds than the North American blackbird and robin, yet they have the same name.

To people of every country the twittering song of the birds is a welcome sound. In Europe early in the spring the cheerful song of the coal-tit and the restrained chirping of the blackbird announce the end of winter. A familiar saying is "One swallow doesn't make a summer," and although this may be true, people still wait longingly for the return of the migrating birds. This is because birds will not return until they sense that the warmer time of the year is beginning and that the change in temperature is quite definite.

When the cuckoo is heard calling his name throughout the land, it is certain that winter is over. The cuckoo's song is heard frequently, but he remains hidden and is only rarely seen. When he flies, he looks very similar to the sparrow hawk. Because of his elusiveness, many tales and legends are told about the cuckoo. One superstition says that if you see a cuckoo you will die within the same year; another says that you should shake your moneybag upon hearing the first cuckoo and it will never be empty for the rest of the year. In fact, in some places, it is believed that the amount of money you have will increase by as many times as the first spring cuckoo calls by the end of the year. The gloomy prophecies of the first superstition have not yet come true for the author of this book, even though he has often seen a cuckoo scurrying secretly from one bush to another or looking for hairy caterpillars in the heath. But whether or not they believe these sayings, people still like to shake their pockets for luck when they hear the first cuckoo.

Birds have many methods of protecting their young. Some brood in caves, others build their nests in hidden spots, and others nest at the very tops of tall trees or in tiny cracks in rocky walls. The birds have many enemies that love to eat fresh eggs or tender fledglings, and they defend their young vigorously. As soon as a cat, weasel, or bird of prey approaches, the birds begin to cry warnings. Then they gather near the enemy and scold him until he seeks refuge in distance. Strangely enough, an attacker once discovered usually abandons his plans, even though his quarry may be lying helpless before his eyes, with the nervous parents far too weak to do him any serious harm. Members of the crow family will fight for their young viciously. If a raven's nest is in danger, the parents come cawing madly and rush at the intruder, stabbing him with their sharp beaks and beating him about the ears with their sturdy wings. Other crows come from all around to help. Screeching loudly in the sky, they fly to attack in defense of the helpless brood and drive the intruder away. But long after the danger is past, there is still great unrest in the crow colony.

Other species of birds rely on deception to get rid of their enemies. When an enemy is near, they land far away from their nest and make their way to it by several byways and detours, or they allow the enemy to come up to the nest and then fall in front of him, dragging themselves off as though seriously hurt. The enemy pursues this seemingly easy catch until it is far away from the nest. Then the parent bird gets up and flies away in perfect health.

Although the birds have clever methods of protecting their young, many fledglings fall victim to storms and vermin and urgently need our protection.

Birds play an important role in the balance of nature. They also provide us with cheerful songs and many relaxing hours of observation. We should protect them gladly.

Tree Sparrow

The tree sparrow is the smaller cousin of the house sparrow, but it is not as tame. It would rather live in orchards and small thickets than near houses. It likes to build its nest in hollows, and from its nest, one can see that the tree sparrow is a weaver. In contrast to the untidy nest of the house sparrow, the nest of the tree sparrow has a roof, as do the nests of the tropical weaver birds. In Italy, tree sparrows build their nests openly in trees, and the similarity of these nests with those of the weaver birds is even greater. Tree sparrows live mainly on seeds and insects, and they feed them to their young when they are brooding. The male is distinguished from the larger male house sparrow by its reddish-brown cap. When the tree sparrows appear in large flocks, they can be very harmful to crops.

The tree sparrow's scientific name is *Passer montanus.* It is found throughout Europe, and closely resembles the North American variety. It was introduced to the United States in 1870 at St. Louis, Missouri. It broods three times a year, and hatches three to seven young.

Call: tsep, tsep, and hweek

House Sparrow - male

Occasionally it is said that someone is as "cocky as a sparrow," and, indeed, the sparrow is very bold. You will find the house sparrow, or hear its chirping, wherever there are people. It has grown so attached to man that it breeds almost exclusively under tiled roofs or in the gaps in house walls. If you leave the kitchen window open, you can almost be sure that the impudent sparrows will immediately come down to inspect the whole kitchen as soon as the door closes behind you. Yet for all its trustfulness, the sparrow remains extremely watchful and wary, and is always prepared for rapid flight when danger threatens. It may feel at home in chicken coops and aviaries (places for keeping birds confined), but its urge for freedom is enormous. A caged sparrow can struggle to death in fear or die of a heart attack, if it notices that it is shut up in a room.

The house sparrow's scientific name is *Passer domesticus*. It is found all over Europe and has been brought to Australia. Americans imported stocks of sparrows to combat harmful insects. It broods four times a year, and hatches three to six young in each brood.

Call: cheep, cheep

House Sparrow - fledgling

Sparrows number among the largest families of the bird world, and because they have a preference for wheat crops, they have become one of the world's most hunted birds. Statisticians have calculated that a pair of sparrows rear up to twenty fledglings in one year. These numerous descendants can and do destroy enormous quantities of seeds. That is why man does not protect the sparrow from harm. It can be pursued and destroyed with any legitimate method that does not cause a painful death. Yet the statisticians are counting only the sparrow's damage to useful plants. The quantities of weed seeds that it eats and the many insects it feeds to its young are never counted, and these insects may very well have caused far more harm to gardens and fields than that caused by the sparrows. All in all, the usefulness and harmfulness of the sparrow equal each other, and thus cancel each other out.

The fledgling sparrow is similarly colored to the female.

Chaffinch - hen

You must have sharp eyes to find a chaffinch nest. Often built into the fork of a branch, its half-spherical nest is almost invisible. The exterior is covered with threads, moss, and lichen, and the nest can hardly be distinguished from the branch itself. The picture here shows the plainly colored female. The male, in all the splendor of his courting display, is shown on the cover. In early spring the male chaffinch begins to sing cheerily, and in this way marks off his territory against his neighbors. During this period the males are very quarrelsome and carry out violent battles for their breeding territory. In autumn after moulting they are not so brightly colored, and they fly peaceably in large flocks across the warmer regions of central and southern Europe.

The chaffinch, *Fringilla coelebs,* is the commonest European member of the finch family. Although it is a grain eater, it also enjoys an occasional insect. It broods once a year and has from three to six young.

Call: didoodoo-dooritchoo, often followed by a hard "pink"

Greenfinch

The greenfinch prefers to breed in thick hedges. It builds its wool-lined nest four feet to nine feet up evergreen trees like the stunted yew tree, the arbor vitae, or the boxwood. The females are a dull olive green, and the males are not much more colorful, but both the male and female have bright yellow feathers on the wings and tail. They feed their young on regurgitated unripe seeds from the crops. When the young fly away, the long white down on their heads makes them look very comical. During the courtship the females, their wings hanging and trembling, beg from the males and are given crops. This behavior exactly mimics the youngsters' begging for food, and is also performed by the other female finches and tits.

Carduelis chloris is found all over Europe. It is a vegetarian, and has two to three broods a year, with from four to six young in each brood.

Call: in flight the male sings choytchoyt-choy-krurr-doodoot

Goldfinch

As soon as the thistles become ripe in late summer the goldfinches fly in large flocks across the countryside. They land in waste areas and rubbish dumps to eat the seeds of the thistles growing there in abundance. Because of this they are also called thistle finches. They are among the most colorful European birds because their main colors of black, yellow, and red are in sharp contrast to the surrounding feathers. In the field it is difficult to distinguish the male from the female. Young goldfinches have gray heads, but as they grow older the intensity of color increases. The males leave the hatching to the hens, which lay three to six pale blue spotted eggs in the softly lined nest.

Carduelis carduelis is widely distributed throughout Europe, northwest Africa, and parts of western Asia, and is a resident in most parts of the British Isles. It spends the winter in central and southern Europe. The goldfinch is also found in small numbers in the northeastern states of America. It feeds on seeds and small insects, and has one to two broods a year, with from three to six young in each brood.

Song: a lively twittering

20 Linnet

The linnet can usually be found in vineyards, railway embankments, and stone piles. In spring the male has his courting colors — a red head and red breast. The hen and chicks have chestnut-brown backs and flecked brownish-gray breasts. In the autumn the male looks much like the female, because the feathers that grow after the summer moult are tipped in gray brown. They fall out during the winter and expose the red color lying underneath. This change of color without a change of feathers occurs with many finches. If the linnet were to go through a full moult, during which all its present feathers would be replaced by new ones, its movement would be affected and its physical strength would be strained beyond all measure. By going through only one change at a time, the linnet still is able to maintain the energy vital to its existence.

Carduelis cannabina breeds throughout Europe, extending as far north as the Arctic Circle. It spends the winter in central and southern Europe, and lives off seeds. It has two broods a year and has four to six young in each brood.

Call: a soft musical twittering

Bullfinch

The female bullfinch lacks the brilliant red breast of the male. Instead, she and the young birds have breasts of gray. During the first moult the breast of the young male is often speckled gray and red for a long time. The bullfinch can be recognized in flight by its brilliant white rump and by its calls of "you" and "bit." Bullfinches are very sociable creatures, and only seldom is a male seen without a female close by. Bullfinches love to live in parks or thickly wooded areas. They build nests of thin twigs and pad them out with hairs and fine roots. They love flower buds, and because they never seem to get enough, they cause serious damage to gardens and orchards.

Pyrrhula pyrrhula breeds in most parts of Europe, and has several varieties. One variety of bullfinch can be found in North America in Alaska on the Nulato and Nunivak Islands. The bullfinch has one to two broods a year, with four to six young in each brood. It eats seeds, buds, and insects. It will sometimes warble sweetly, but has no full song.

24 Serin

You can find this little finch in orchards, parks, and even in gardens. While the female sits brooding on the nest in trees or hedges, the male flutters around like a bat, uttering his mating call continually. When garden flowers have withered and the seeds come, whole families of serins arrive crying their clear call of "girlit, girlit," for unripe seeds are their favorite dish. The fledglings, too, are fed a vegetarian diet of regurgitated seeds from the crops. The brow, breast, and rump of the male serins are yellow; the hens are more plainly colored but are more noticeably striped. The hens hatch their eggs in twelve to fourteen days, all the time being fed by the males. After that, both parents help with the upbringing of their children.

Serinus serinus breeds in Europe, Asia Minor, and Africa. It has two broods a year, each of which has three to five young. The serin lives on seeds.

Yellowhammer - male

The bird most commonly found near villages, in shrubberies, and at the edges of fields and woods is the yellowhammer. In the winter it comes in large flocks to the villages and sometimes takes refuge in barns. Yellowhammers often come in the company of other finches. They have gray feathers until spring, when their courting colors become visible, and then the male has a golden yellow head. Another way to identify the yellowhammer is by its chestnut-brown rump. Usually the male sings from a high perch or withered branch where he can be seen from a long distance away. When he sings he seems to be saying "hee, hee, hee, do I love thee." With the yellowhammer too, the female must do all the brooding.

Emberiza citrinella is widely distributed in the British Isles and spends the winter in central and southern Europe. The yellowhammer is a member of the bunting family. Varieties of buntings are distributed throughout North America.

Song: vee vee vee-vay vay vay-tsee

Yellowhammer - hen

The yellowhammer builds a shapeless nest out of roots, stalks, and stems in low thickets and bushes, but seldom on the ground. Into it she lays three to five dark-spotted white eggs. She hatches them out alone in eleven to thirteen days, and then both parents take part in the upbringing of their offspring. Depending on the weather, the young leave the nest after nine to fourteen days, but continue to be fed until the mother has to concentrate on the second brood. Hatching is an extremely strenuous business for the older birds, and their beautiful feathers are completely ruined by having to search for food. Thus, the brooding period is followed by a moulting period during which all the feathers are changed. This happens in such a way that the bird can still fly, but it is capable of only very limited movement. The birds prefer to stay hidden during this period.

Yellowhammer - fledgling

Some birds are called nest-chickens, because they creep blind and naked from the egg. For the first few days they have to be continuously protected and warmed by a parent. Through scientific experiment it has been discovered that the skin on the stomachs of brooding birds is considerably warmer than the skin on other parts of their bodies. Bird parents usually change shifts every few hours during brooding, but the yellowhammer and other finch hens often have to hatch their young alone, though the male does help with feeding. The young birds lie quietly in the nest when their parents are away, but if a parent bird comes to the edge of the nest, the young beg from it with wide-open beaks. It puts the food in the nearest mouth, and often a weak young bird will starve to death because it did not beg enough food.

32

Bee-Eater

Whenever this bird is seen in northern Europe people think it is an escaped cagebird. Bee-eaters can be found in the north, but they are very rare. An estimated twenty-five pairs or so have been seen in Germany, and recently near Hamburg two pairs have bred in holes they made themselves in steep slopes. Unfortunately, even though it is a protected bird, the bee-eater is often shot down because of its beauty, and its nest is also destroyed by bee-keepers. It beats its wings rapidly when flying, and soars in circular patterns. The bee is its main source of food, but it also eats wasps, dragonflies, and beetles, and swoops down and catches them in flight. The bird sanctuary at Ludwigsburg, Germany, is now engaged in praiseworthy attempts to resettle the bee-eater in large quantities in Germany. For this purpose the birds are bred in large open-air aviaries and then set free. This photograph was taken in the Ludwigsburg aviary.

Merops apiaster breeds in southwest and southern Europe, northwest Africa, Asia Minor, Iraq, and Persia. It is an occasional visitor to northern Europe, including Britain. It spends its winters in Africa.

Call: qui-ick qui-ick

Hoopoe

Today the hoopoe is found mainly in the warmer countries of Europe. It lives mostly in pastures, and picks dung-beetles and insect larvae out of dried cow-pads with its long, slightly curved beak. When it feeds it continually raises the head-comb that it usually wears flat and tilted back. There has been a decreasing number of large pasture areas in Europe with the development of new, more technical methods of raising cattle, and as a result, many of the hoopoe's breeding grounds and original sources of food have been destroyed. In northern Europe the hoopoe is very shy, and nests in hidden hollows and cracks. But in southern Europe it even dares to come into villages, and often lays its six eggs between the stumps in piles of wood. If an enemy approaches the nest, the young birds lift their rears and shoot a load of stinking droppings into the intruder's face.

Upupa epops winters in Africa. Its low mating call of "hoopoopoo" is heard far and wide.

Wryneck

The wryneck is very seldom seen, but its nasal call of "gaygaygay" is heard in every orchard in the spring, sung by both male and female in front of the nest. The wryneck likes to turn its head through an angle of 180 degrees, and does so by moving its extended neck like a snake. Unusual as this well-camouflaged bird is, its nesting habits are even more unusual. The wryneck does not build a nest. It lays its eggs in natural holes and hollows, only after throwing out any nesting material left there by another bird. The wryneck often comes close to houses, but the coloring of its feathers can hardly be distinguished from the branch it is sitting on. Should an enemy approach, the wryneck does not seek refuge in flight as other birds do. Instead, it remains firmly seated, and relies on its camouflage and neck movements for safety.

Jynx torquilla, a member of the woodpecker family, can be found in the east and southeast of England. It winters in the Tropics, and its major source of food is the ant. The hen broods once a year and lays seven to ten eggs.

Skylark

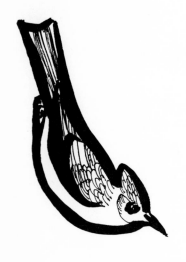

Not until the skylark soars into the sky on the wings of its song does spring begin in Europe. The male skylark seldom will sing from the ground. Generally it rises, singing, and climbs so high into the heavens that it can hardly be seen with the naked eye. Then, still singing, it sinks slowly to its nest, dropping the last thirty to sixty feet in silence. Even when you have seen the landing spot clearly and have carefully sought it out, you will not find the skylark there. It has quite secretly slipped away. At first the female remains motionless on the nest when approached, and then moves quietly away, unnoticed, when you come too close. The young leave the nest even before they can fly.

Alauda arvensis can be found throughout Europe, and up to 1907 was occasionally seen in North America. It winters in the Mediterranean, and has two broods a year, hatching three to six young at each brooding.

Song: trilling, whistling notes

Crested Lark

A brooding crested lark is hard to find, even though it builds its nest quite openly on the ground near paths and rubbish dumps. The many dark spots and streaks on its feathers merge strongly and blend with the colors of its surroundings. It can only be seen clearly when it moves and raises its pointed crest in excitement, calling "dree dree dreer" as it flies away. The crested lark prefers to live in barren areas in the plains, and in winter comes right into the villages. Previously it lived off the remains left by horses, and in the 1930's it was feared that a decrease in the number of horses would lead to the disappearance of the crested lark. And, in fact, it has died out in many parts of Germany since the war.

Galerida cristata is a resident of northern Europe. It broods two times a year, producing from four to five young, and lives off seeds and insects. Its song is similar to that of the skylark, but shorter.

Swallow

Because they have short legs and can only hop around clumsily on the ground, swallows have given themselves up almost entirely to a life in the air. They land only when they want mud for their nests. They mix this mud with saliva, and out of it they carefully make semi-spherical nests on the rafters in stalls and barns. The hen lays her eggs onto the lining of feathers. Only the mother broods, but after twelve to eighteen days the young birds hatch and are looked after by both parents. They leave the nest some twenty days later, but are still fed for some time. At night the family gathers together in the warm nest. Swallows even drink in flight by snatching up water in their lower beaks.

Hirundo rustica, a close relative of the North American barn swallow, can be found in most parts of Europe, and related species occur in East Asia. It winters in India and Africa. It broods two to three times a year, hatching from three to six young, and lives on flies.

Song: a musical twittering

House Martin

The house martin is a relative of the swallow, but can be easily distinguished from the swallow by its shorter forked tail and white rump. Its throat is also white, not red like the swallow's. The house martin can also be recognized by its nest. Usually, the rounded, almost totally closed nest is built under an overhanging roof or in some other rain-protected spot on the outside of a house. No farmer ever harms a martin because disturbing a martin's nest is supposed to bring bad luck. Martins, like swallows, live almost exclusively on flying insects. They prefer to eat houseflies, which they catch by flying into high air currents where these insects are most numerous. Because they can find flies only where there is no strong wind, it is said that the weather can be predicted by the way martins fly.

Delichon urbica is distributed throughout Europe and western Asia, and related species can be found from northwest Africa to Japan. Varieties of this species can also be found in North America. In the autumn the house martins gather in large flocks and perch on electricity wires before their migration to Africa for the winter. Its song is more twittery than that of the swallow.

Call: a hard, gritty chirrup

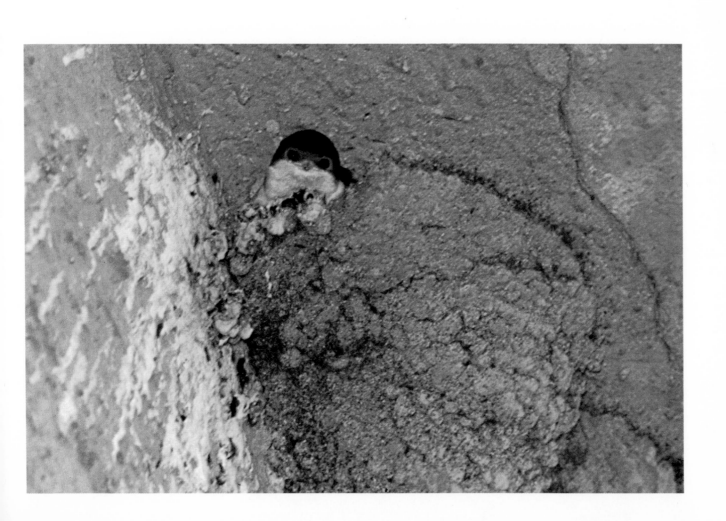

Carrion Crow

Although it prefers to nest in high trees and sleeps there in large flocks when the breeding season is over, the carrion crow is found predominantly in fields and near villages. It is hunted because it preys on mice, snails, insects, and young birds. It is clever enough to distinguish a harmless wanderer from a stalking hunter, however, and always stays out of shooting range. A farmer plowing his field is often followed by crows, because the plow turns up the cockchafer grubs and mice that they like to eat. The carrion crow cares for its brood and defends it vigorously. It will attack intruders from a great height, stabbing them with its beak as it flies at them again and again.

Corvus corone is closely related to the hooded crow. It lives in western Europe, and another race lives in Asia. It brings up from three to six young a year.

Call: a deep "caw"

Hooded Crow

The hooded crow differs from its closest relative, the carrion crow, only in coloring. During the summer it is found in the eastern parts of Europe, but in winter it will move as far west as France. Like the other species of crows, it seeks food in rubbish dumps, and is sometimes called the scavenging crow. Its size, behavior patterns, song, and chosen residences are all exactly like those of the carrion crow. The hooded crow sometimes crossbreeds with the carrion crow, and their offspring have every possible variation on the colors of the parent birds. Crows begin their mating season in late winter and stay faithful to their mates throughout their lives. The crow's call is usually harsh and noisy, but in mating season it changes to a cheerful, ventriloquist-like chattering call. In captivity, young crows can learn to talk.

Corvus corone cornix can be found mainly in parts of central and eastern Europe. It breeds in Ireland, the Isle of Man, Scotland, and occasionally in England. A few hooded crows have been found near Iceland and Greenland. It will consume anything that is edible.

Great Tit

Even in the depths of winter the male will sing as soon as the sun breaks through the clouds. When it is not the mating season, the great tits join together with large flocks of woodpeckers, nuthatches, and other titmice to roam the woods and orchards searching for food. They love to hang upside down from branches. In spring the pale-feathered hens beg food from the males exactly as the young birds do — they crouch on a branch with their wings drooping and trembling, and chirrup pleadingly like a baby. Their nests are built at many different heights, and are built by the hen without any help from the male. The male accompanies her on her flights, but she must also do all the brooding alone. Only after the young have hatched will the male help.

Parus major can be found all over Europe. It winters in the Mediterranean and France, and occasionally in Germany. The chickadee is the most familiar member of the titmouse family found in North America. The great tit has one brood a year with from seven to thirteen young.

Call: tsitsibay

Blue Tit

The blue tit is the most colorful of the titmice, and is as lively as a cricket. It can often be found hanging upside down from a leaf looking for butterfly eggs, or flying to a gnarled tree trunk in search of beetle larvae and butterfly pupae. Upon finding them, it picks them out and consumes them with delight. If you have sharp eyes you might be able to watch it holding a pupa in its claw and chewing it up bit by bit. Blue tits are very busy during the mating season because a hen can lay up to fourteen eggs, which means there are many mouths to feed. The parents have very little spare time because their young cry almost uninterruptedly for food, and they must be fed continuously with caterpillars and spiders.

Parus caeruleus is found throughout Europe, and winters in central and southern Europe.

Call: a scolding tsee tsee tsit

Marsh Tit

The least colorful of the tits is the marsh tit. It has gray-brown plumage and a black cap, and could easily be mistaken for the male blackcap if its behavior patterns were not so completely different. While the quiet blackcap likes to live in hidden spots, the noisy marsh tit is always dashing around, singing "tsipya" frequently and sharply. Marsh tits are usually found in pairs, hanging upside down in the foliage looking for small caterpillars and butterfly eggs. The willow tit is still native to Germany and has coloring very similar to the marsh tit. The willow tit has a smooth black cap and prefers damp areas while the marsh tit is found almost everywhere, but these two can only be distinguished by their calls.

Parus palustris is distributed throughout England and Wales. It spends the winter in Germany, eats insects, and raises six to ten young once a year.

Song: a rattling chepchepchep...

Nuthatch

This pretty, softly colored bird is also called a wood-pecker-titmouse. It is the only one of the European birds that can run down a tree headfirst. It searches tree trunks for insects, pupae, and eggs untiringly, usually beginning at the base of the trunk and climbing it in a spiral. When finished, it flies on to the base of the next trunk. If the nuthatch finds a hollow already occupied, it throws out all the nesting material of the occupant and does not hesitate to destroy the eggs too. Then it seals up the entrance with clay and saliva until it is so small that only the nuthatch can get in. The rightful owner is left out in the cold, for the clay soon hardens and cannot be broken open. The nut-hatches always defend their new homes vigorously.

Sitta europaea resides throughout Europe, and its various species extend as far east as Japan. Varieties of the nuthatch can be found throughout North America. In the warmer months the nuthatch lives on insects, and in the winter it lives on seeds. It has one brood a year of four to eight young.

Song: ti tweet tweet and veehay veehay veehay

Blackbird - male

Thirty years ago blackbirds were shy woodland birds that only ventured out as far as the gardens and parks of suburbs. Today you could call the blackbird a town bird. It makes its home primarily in gardens and lawns, and builds its nest very close to human habitats, often right in front of the balcony window. Its closer contact with man has led it to be careless in its building of nests, and as a result, many young blackbirds fall prey to cats. The arrival of the blackbirds from their winter migration is a very pleasant time, for the jet black, yellow-billed males sing their liquid songs from morning to evening. They often weave snatches of other birds' songs into their own melodies, sometimes even including a human whistle which they learn from the other males.

Turdus merula nests everywhere in Europe, and often spends winter in the towns. It is a member of the thrush family, and is in no way related to the North American blackbird. It utters a repeated call of "tchook" at sunset.

Song: a mellow fluting

Blackbird - hen

The hen blackbird differs from the male with his black coat and yellow beak by having brown plumage, a spotted throat, and a brown beak. While the males defend the breeding areas with their loud songs and occasional display battles, the females are much more aggressive. They often fight violently with their rivals, oblivious to all that surrounds them. They are also prepared to kill other birds' young in the nest, and even eat them if they are small enough. Their fighting habits in no way alter the large population of the town blackbirds, because they often hatch out six young birds three times a year. But other songsters, especially insect-eaters, suffer, and they finally retreat when the blackbirds become too numerous.

Turdus merula always stays very close to her home.

Blackbird - fledgling

The blackbird's nest is made of twigs mixed with earth, and is lined with soft stems. Into it the hen lays three to six blue-green, reddish-brown-spotted eggs. You can often find blackbird nests at the end of February during brooding time when the hen does not dare leave the nest because the eggs would perish. Eleven to fourteen days later, the naked blind birds hatch and are fed by their parents on slugs and worms. Even though they are blind, the fledglings notice when something approaches the nest, and if you touch the edge of the nest they stretch towards you begging and shrieking loudly. Soon their quills sprout and their eyes open. Then they are in a position to distinguish what is approaching the nest, and begin to beg if it is their parents or a decoy. But if it is anything else, they silently crouch low in the nest, or if they are big enough, they fly away.

The blackbird fledglings eat insects, worms, and snails.

Wheatear

The wheatear makes its home in wasteland areas, heathlands (open uncultivated land), pastures, and occasionally in vineyards. There it likes to sit on heaps of stones, and less frequently on fenceposts and low trees. Whenever it bobs up and down it spreads its tail and shows its white markings. These markings easily identify the wheatear in flight, as shown in the sketch. The male during the mating season has black wings and ear caps, a white stripe across its eyes, and a blue-gray back, but otherwise it looks very similar to the hen in our picture. Wheatears nest in piles of stones, hollows, and even in rabbit breeding grounds. Although they are not very shy, they avoid cultivated land areas.

Oenanthe oenanthe can be found in the northern and central areas of Europe. It is a summer visitor to England, and winters in the African Steppes. A larger race of wheatear breeds in Greenland and Iceland, and an Asiatic species sometimes reaches North America by migrating to Alaska in the summer. The North American variety is very similar to the European variety. The wheatear produces four to six young a year.

Song: like that of the lark, but shorter

Redstart - male

Soon after he returns from his winter sojourn in Africa, the male redstart begins to search out a home for himself. Holes in vineyard walls, hollows in trees, niches in walls, and nesting boxes suit him very well. When he has finally found the right spot, he sings inside the hollow or repeatedly flies back and forth to the nesting place, spreading out his rust-red tail. In this way he tells his wife the location of the new home. The redstart likes to live in sunny areas at the edges of woods, in large orchards of old trees, or in vineyards, and prefers to sing from the thick branches of old trees. Its song is very changeable, often beginning with short, flute-like tones followed by several short trills.

Phoenicurus phoenicurus is found throughout Europe, and breeds from northern Norway to Spain and Sicily. It winters in the Mediterranean.

Redstart - hen

The color of the female redstart is a modest mixture of brown and gray. The male and female have only the rust-red tail in common. This tail serves as a warning flag, and as a recognition and code signal. When excited, the redstart bobs up and down with its tail trembling. The positioning of the tail, the frequency of the bobs, and its harsh call of "hit-teck-teck," are all signals that are understood by fellow redstarts. If a cat is creeping around the garden, if an owl is sitting on a branch, or if a weasel appears, the redstarts come immediately to chase away the enemy with wild clamorings. They fly very close to him and the closer they get, the more they hop around. And the more they hop around, the less chance the enemy has to catch them. In addition, they are so wary that they can escape at the slightest sign of attack.

The redstart raises three to eight young in one brood.

Although the redstart is primarily a hollow-dweller, it will make its nest in shallow holes when nothing else is available. The nest in our picture is built on the ground beneath a pile of twigs. The hen hatches out the eggs alone in about fourteen days. The young are fed insects, small caterpillars, beetle larvae, and many spiders. As long as the fledglings are still blind, they beg from everything that moves past the nest. Sometimes they have been so disturbed by the vibrations of a moving object that they have chirped and given away the nest's location. Later, when they begin to see, they recognize their parents and react to a stranger by withdrawing far into the nest and lying absolutely still. Cats and martens are frequent nest robbers, and steal many young birds from the nests by fishing them out with their claws.

The fledgling redstart is spotted light and dark.

Black Redstart - fledgling

Compared to his cousin, the redstart, the black redstart is gray and somber colored. Only its tail is rust-red, and this color extends as far as the central feathers. The hen's coloring is similar to that of the redstart hen but is more slate gray and has no brown tinges. Black redstarts bob up and down more often than redstarts do, and like to sit on rooftops and television aerials. They build their large nests in hollows and nesting boxes, and also in slits in walls and under roof tiles. They lay four to six pure white eggs onto a bed of feathers and animal hair. Only the female broods. In summer, even before dawn, the black redstart sings its song. It sounds rather like "didididit-tschrch-dididid-it," and can be compared to the sound of a flag squeaking on its pole. The males also sing in autumn.

Phoenicurus ochruros can be found throughout Europe. It winters in the Mediterranean.

Bluethroat

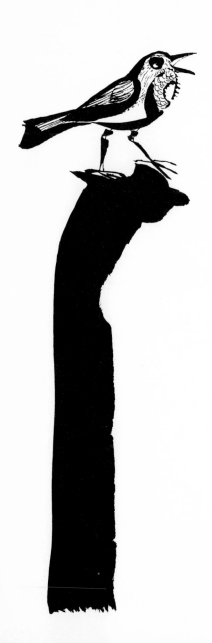

The bluethroat is found mainly in boggy areas, and prefers to perch on willow branches and other shrubs. Although it is quite rare in southern Europe, it is often found in northern Europe. The male, singing from a prominent perch, usually begins with a high, increasingly quick "dip-dip-dip-dip," followed by imitations of other birds' songs. It often sings as it flies into the air with its reddish-brown tail outspread. Only the male has the shining blue throat. The German subspecies has a white star in the center of the throat, and the Scandinavian subspecies has a red star. The hen has a white throat edged in blue gray or gray brown. The young birds have brown tails and are brown and gray spotted.

Luscinia svevica breeds from Scandinavia eastwards into Siberia, and winters in northern Africa and southern Asia. The red-spotted bluethroat can be found in western Alaska. The bluethroat eats insects, and has five to six young once a year.

Robin

The robin with its brown feathers, shining red breast, and large, expressive eyes may seem gentle, but it is a bird that defends its territory very seriously against intruders. It marks its territory with its loud song, and rushes angrily at any rival who attempts to enter its kingdom. It often has violent battles with other birds. If a robin is kept in a cage, it must not be put in with any other bird because another bird could easily fall prey to the robin's jealousy. Robins are very trusting of man — they have even been known to come and sit very close to a person on a park bench. Whenever insects are disturbed from their resting spots in the shrubbery, robins soon turn up to catch them. The female robin will often join the male in song.

Erithacus rubecula is a resident throughout Britain and Ireland. It winters in the Mediterranean, but if the winter is mild, many of the older birds will stay in their homes instead of migrating. The European robin is a great deal different from the North American robin, *Turdus migratorius,* which is actually a member of the blackbird family.

Robin - fledgling

The similar coloring of the cock and hen robin makes them hardly distinguishable from each other, but the coloring of the fledgling is completely different. Its speckled coat is similar to that of the young redstart but it does not have a red tail. Young robins often leave the nest before they are fledged — have acquired the feathers necessary for flight. The robin's nest is built on the ground beneath tree roots, in other hollows, or in well-protected ground dips. The coloring of the fledgling is excellent camouflage against the surrounding brown foliage. The mother, too, relies on her coloring for camouflage, and at the approach of an enemy presses herself close to the ground so that her red breast is no longer visible. At the very last moment she flies straight into the intruder's face.

Song: high notes and sparkling phrases

Cuckoo

The gray-brown feathered cuckoo is a parasite. The hen does not make her own nest. She prefers to lay her eggs in the nest of another bird whose eggs resemble hers in size and color. She will lay up to twelve eggs in separate nests and leave them to the care of the hosts. The young cuckoo hatches much earlier than the host's eggs, and a cruel instinct urges it to throw the other eggs out of the nest immediately. It grows quickly and is fed untiringly by its foster parents, even though it is soon bigger than they are. Once the author found a robin's nest underneath some bilberry bushes. Two cuckoo's eggs had been smuggled into the nest, and when the first cuckoo hatched, he threw the other eggs out of the nest. But the nest was on the ground, and the rejected brood was now lying at the edge of the shrubbery. The returning mother found her eggs and continued to hatch them outside the nest. One night, however, a stray cat came and destroyed this unusual family. The photograph was taken the evening before this catastrophe.

Cuculus canorus can be found in most parts of Europe. It lives off insects, and prefers to eat hairy caterpillars. Ten species and subspecies of the cuckoo are found in North America, and these varieties build their own nests and rear their own young.

Call: "cuck-oo," sometimes combined with an angry "kow kow kow"

Blackcap

The black cap of the male gave this breed its name. The hen and the young birds — which leave the nest before they are fully fledged — have red caps. The blackcap's nest is made of small branches and roots, and is loosely positioned low in the bushes. When an enemy approaches, the hen rushes out and flops on the ground as though her wings are broken, and then limps away slowly but very noticeably. The enemy is usually taken in by this trick and follows the hen, thinking her to be an easy catch. She leads him far away from the nest, and then suddenly flies off. Such deception is almost always successful and saves the helpless chicks.

Sylvia atricapilla can be found in Europe from Norway southwards. It winters in the Mediterranean. The blackcap raises from three to six young. It lives off insects, and in the autumn eats fruit and elderberries. The blackcap's chatty song includes other birds' songs, and finishes these with a flute-like somersault of notes.

Spotted Flycatcher

Although most of its feathers are a subdued shade of gray brown, the spotted flycatcher is a very noticeable bird. It likes to sit on withered branches and observe its surroundings. It catches gnats and other insects in flight, and usually eats them while still flying. As it eats it snaps its beak loudly, and this is a sure sign by which to recognize it. Typical of the spotted flycatcher, too, are the dives it makes from high perches. It is often found in thinly wooded areas, in gardens, and near farms, where it hunts flies. Its nest is made of moss and cobwebs, and is lined with fine grass and hair. It is built at a medium height and found in slits or on ledges of walls, buildings, rocks, and trees. In northern Europe the spotted flycatcher has only one brood a year, but in the warmer south it has two broods, each brood having from three to six young. The young, too, are gray, but their upper sides are spotted dark and light brown, and their spotted breasts appear to be flaky. They beg very loudly.

Muscicapa striata is distributed throughout Europe and winters in the African Tropics. The European flycatchers are not related to the North American flycatchers, which are members of the *Tyrannidae* family.

Call: a thin "zee," accompanied by a loud alarm of "tuck tuck" when danger approaches

Hedge Sparrow

The hedge sparrow or dunnock leads a sheltered life, and the male is seen very seldom. He usually sings his humble song from the end of a branch in a bush. Even when seeking food, the hedge sparrow rarely leaves its own territory. It prefers to get its insects from blackberry and pine bushes, from bushes around fields, and from plants in the cultivated areas of churchyards and gardens. The nest is built of twigs, and is lined with moss, hair, and sometimes even with feathers. It is found in the thickest bush, usually not more than three to five feet off the ground. In winter the hedge sparrow moves to the warmer areas of central and western Europe, but it prefers to live in the Mediterranean areas. At night during migration you can often hear the high "tsit" and metallic "dididi" of its song.

Prunella modularis can be found throughout Europe. It has two broods a year, with from three to six young in each brood.

Song: a simple burst of notes vaguely similar to that of the wren

Tree Pipit

An enthralling song can often be heard in parks, forest clearings, and fruit plantations where there are old trees. If you follow the sound, you will come upon a bird rising into the sky singing like a lark. As it sinks slowly down with wings widely spread, its song is still loud. This is the tree pipit. It is much smaller than a lark, and differs from it also in the relationship of body size to wingspread. The wings of the tree pipit are much larger than those of the skylark. Its song is also different, and the tree pipit does not fly as high as the lark. Its nest is built out of moss and reeds, and is hidden in the grass. When feeding the young, the adults do not fly directly to the nest as most other birds do. Instead, they land some considerable distance from it and then creep up to it, thus keeping its location a secret from its enemies.

Anthus trivialis makes its home throughout Europe. It has two broods a year and has from four to six young in each brood. It lives on insects and snails.

Call: a penetrating "tsi"

Meadow Pipit

The meadow pipit can hardly be distinguished from its cousin, the tree pipit. Its hind claw is longer and its breast is not as yellow as the tree pipit's, but its upper half is more olive green. It is easiest to recognize a meadow pipit by the area in which it lives. It is found in moorlands, coastal dunes, marshes, and meadows. When mating, it flies up singing from a high perch, never rising very high. Then, still singing, it falls like a parachute back to its original spot. Another way to distinguish the meadow pipit from the tree pipit is by its song. When it rises into the air the meadow pipit sings a quickening call of "dip-dip-dip," and during its fall this song becomes an equally quick "tsi-tsi-tsi-tsi-tsi-tsi-tsi."

Anthus pratensis is common to the northern parts of Europe, and is also found in Iceland. A variety of pipit can be found in North America, especially near the Atlantic Coast. The meadow pipit winters in the warmer parts of central and southern Europe, and lives on insects, spiders, snails, and seeds.

White Wagtail

Although members of the wagtail species live near flowing water and are sometimes called "water wagtails," the white wagtail is found nearly everywhere. It particularly likes to live on farms, and spends much of its time catching the flies found buzzing around cattle. It is a lively bird, and not at all shy. It has a long, flicking tail, and often will scurry around between a person's feet. But the wagtail is very wary, and is always prepared to escape any danger. If an enemy approaches, the wagtail sounds a loud "tsilip" and flies away. In winter the wagtails migrate from northern and central Europe to Africa, and there they can be found by every stream of water, running around under the crocodile's nose. They have even been seen in desert areas, where they like to follow the nomads.

Motacilla alba can be found throughout Europe, as far north as Britain. It is an occasional visitor to Greenland and northern Quebec. The white wagtail has two broods a year and has four to seven young in each brood. It lives on insects and molluscs.

Song: a twittering of notes and calls of "tsilip"

Blue-headed Wagtail

The blue-headed wagtail spends much more time in wet areas than does the white wagtail. It can often be found seeking food in grazing areas and marshes. It eats mainly snails, caterpillars, and other small insects. It also eats flies, and catches them by jumping quickly into the air. The bird can be easily identified by its yellow belly. There are many kinds of subspecies of blue-headed wagtail, and these can be identified by the coloring of the upper part of the male during the mating season. Out of the mating season the males of this species are similar to the hens in coloring. They have a yellowish gray-brown coloring on the upper side and a paler yellow coloring on the underside. The young birds have a pale gray-brown back, and a clay-colored underside with pale flecks on the breast.

Motacilla flava is found in most parts of Europe. It has one brood a year of five to six young.

Song: a muted twittering

Great Grey Shrike

Although shrikes belong to the sparrow family, their behavior is more similar to that of the birds of prey. Above all, the great grey shrike moves like a falcon. It prefers smaller birds and mice as its main food, but will also eat insects and frogs. You can often see the shrike sitting on a high lookout searching the ground for food. Then, without warning, it drops down with a sure aim onto its prey. Its enemies are the falcons, and the shrike always watches the sky very carefully and hides as soon as a falcon appears on the horizon. It likes to wedge its larger catches of food into tree forks and eat them in small doses. But it also sticks them on thorns, as does its cousin, the red-backed shrike. Our color photo shows a great grey shrike in its winter quarters in the Sudan.

Lanius excubitor winters in central and southern Europe, and also in northern Africa. There are eight species and subspecies found in North America. The great grey shrike breeds three to eight young a year. Its call is harsh, and it likes to imitate the calls of other birds.

Starling

With its cheerful songs and imitations of other birds' songs, the starling is the clown of the bird world. It is loved as an announcer of spring, but is hated in autumn when giant flocks of starlings attack the vineyards, for they can destroy a whole crop in a short time. Today man has found a humane way of keeping the birds off the fruits — the warning cries of starlings have been tape-recorded, and they are played at night near the reed beds or park trees where starlings sleep in groups of several thousand. On hearing the warning cries the whole flock flies away in fear and begins its migration to the south a little too soon. There, although they have lived the whole summer mainly on insects, they eat the grapes and olives, and are therefore hunted a great deal.

Sturnus vulgaris is distributed throughout Europe and North America. It was originally brought to the United States from England in the 19th century and set loose in New York. Starlings live on insects and fruit. They have two broods a year, with from three to eight young in each brood. Its call is a harsh "churr."

Song: a mixture of clicks, whistles, and notes copied from songs of other birds

Collared Turtle Dove

With each year civilization moves farther into the bird's living areas and takes control. While the majority of birds have difficulty adjusting to this and many birds are dying out, the turtle dove has recently carried out a triumphal procession through Europe. Although it was originally found in the Near East and the Balkans, it has now increased its breeding areas to cover the northwest where at first it was welcomed as an addition to the bird world we know. Since then, however, it has become almost a torment in towns and parks, and man has been forced to reduce its numbers by hunting it or by removing its eggs. In spring the male receives his beautiful mating colors, and in early morning he can be heard singing his deep "coo-coo-coo" from high trees or telegraph poles. The collared turtle dove flies by rising into the air in a steep line and then sailing down with its wings and tail outspread.

Varieties of *Streptopelia decaocto* can be found in southeastern Europe, Africa, central Asia, and the Orient. One variety has become naturalized in North America near Los Angeles, California. The collared turtle dove lives off seeds and plants.

Quail

In previous years the quail's song of "pickwerwick pickwerwick" could be heard from spring through to summer, but today the quail is rarer and is hardly ever heard. Its decreasing numbers could be caused by man's new methods of planting crops or by his intensive hunting of wild birds in the Mediterranean lands during migration. Quails lead a secluded life in cornfields and neglected meadows. They breed in shallow hollows in the ground. The young leave the nest as soon as they have hatched, but are fed by their parents until they are fully fledged. Otherwise, quails live individually, and only form flocks to migrate. Their bodies are heavy and clumsy, and they have to beat their wings rapidly when flying. During migration they fly mostly by night, and are exhausted when they finally reach the African coast. There they are met by hunters with clubs, and are beaten down in enormous numbers and taken to market.

Coturnix coturnix is a member of the pheasant family, and can be found throughout Europe. The North American quail is a member of the grouse family. The quail has one or two broods a year with from seven to twelve young in each brood.

Stone Curlew

The stone curlew nests in the heath, in bare sand-dunes, in stony areas, and sometimes also on cultivated land. It is at home throughout central Europe. Few people will ever see the curlew because it is shy and lives hidden away, only emerging at dusk to hunt food. It sees extremely well with its large yellow eyes, and catches snakes and frogs even in the dark. Often at night you can hear its loud voice wailing "ku-ri" or shrilly crying "ki-rrr-uh." When resting it stretches out its legs horizontally and lays its head on the ground. It can make itself quite flat when it wants to be invisible. Because of its light brown and white striped plumage it can hardly be distinguished from the ground, and people are often surprised when a large bird with white bands suddenly flies up and away from under their feet.

Burhinus oedicnemus is found in most European countries, and winters in the Mediterranean and Africa.

White Stork

Recently the number of storks in Europe, particularly in Germany, has begun to decrease alarmingly. One definite cause of this is the drying out of marshes and reedlands. Telegraph and telephone wires are also a hazard for storks, and many young storks fly into them and break their necks and wings. There are probably other reasons for their decreasing numbers, too. Even attempts by bird wardens to resettle these birds have had little success. We can only hope that this decrease is actually a change or shift in their nesting habits, as has already occurred with other birds. Storks remain faithful married couples throughout their lives. In spring the male is the first to return from their winter home. He repairs the nest and then waits for his wife, greeting her tenderly when she arrives. In autumn the storks form large flocks and migrate together to Africa.

Ciconia ciconia is distributed throughout Europe. About twenty species of stork are known. One species can be found in North America where it breeds chiefly in Florida. The white stork eats insects, frogs, and reptiles, and breeds two to three young a year.

NATURE AND MAN

Books in This Series

AMONG THE PLAINS INDIANS, a fictional account based on the actual travels of two explorers who observed American Indian life in the 1830's, features illustrations by artists George Catlin and Karl Bodmer.

AQUARIUM FISH from Around the World presents an exciting picture of the varied species of fish that inhabit the miniature world of an aquarium.

BIRDS OF THE WORLD in Field and Garden combines colorful photographs and an informative text to describe some of the world's most interesting birds.

CREATURES OF POND AND POOL describes many of the beautiful and unusual creatures—frogs, water snakes, salamanders, aquatic insects—that live in and around fresh-water ponds.

DOMESTIC PETS describes the special characteristics of the animals which can live comfortably and happily with man, including several kinds of dogs, cats, birds, monkeys, reptiles, and fish.

WILD ANIMALS OF AFRICA takes the reader on a safari with German naturalist Klaus Paysan, who tells of his adventures in Africa and describes the living habits of the continent's most fascinating animals.

These fact-filled books contain more than fifty four-color plates and over 100 pages. Printed on high quality paper and reinforced bound, these books will add an exciting new dimension to any collection.

For more information about these and other quality books for young people, please write to

LERNER PUBLICATIONS COMPANY

241 First Avenue North, Minneapolis, Minnesota 55401

Larva of the *Acilius* Diving Beetle, a photograph from *Creatures of Pond and Pool*

24951

598.2 Paysan, Klaus
PAY
        Birds of the world
           in field and garden